LLC

A Complete Guide To Limited Liability Companies And Setting Up Your Own LLC

Table of Contents

Introduction

Thank you for taking the time to pick up this book about limited liability companies (LLCs).

This book aims to serve as a guide to LLCs, and will take you step by step through the process of establishing one, as well as educating you on the considerations you should take before deciding upon an LLC structure.

In the following chapters you will learn about the different company structures available, and the pros and cons of each. For many, the LLC structure, or a variation thereof, will be the most suitable.

This book also covers what you need to do and consider with regards to taxation, maintaining your LLC, your legal obligations, and banking as an LLC.

Once again, thank you for choosing this book. I hope you find it to be helpful in your pursuit of successfully starting and operating a limited liability company!

Chapter 1: What Are the Options?

LLC is a very common abbreviation today, following the name of so many companies that we might expect that the average individual knows what it means. Of course, you probably know that it stands for "limited liability company," but what does that entail?

A limited liability company is one of a variety of options for business structures that you have when you are creating a start-up company with just yourself or yourself and a few partners as owners. It began in Germany with the GmbH, or *Gesellschaft mit beschränkter Haftung,* which means literally, "company with limited liability." It later expanded as a business model to the United States as the LLC.

There are a few other options you have when creating your business in terms of business model. Your other options include sole proprietorship, cooperative, C corporation (otherwise known as simply "corporation"), partnership, and S corporation. To more deeply appreciate the advantages of an LLC, let us look at the various other options with their pros and cons. Then we will see how they compare to the LLC in the next chapter.

Sole Proprietorship

If you establish a sole proprietorship, you are the sole owner of the business you have created. You are responsible for the assets and all profits and losses. This unincorporated type of business model will sometimes run under a fictitious name, or a DBA (doing business as). The business is taxed on the individual owner's personal tax form.

The advantages of this model include the following:

1) Tax preparation is simpler with there being only one tax form to fill out for both the individual and the business. All profit and loss information is contained on the individual's tax form.

2) The individual owner has complete control over the business. Conflict among partners is not a problem, and decisions are streamlined by the autocratic process of the single business owner's responses and choices in various situations.

3) This is the most inexpensive type of business to form. There is very little paperwork required to set up a sole proprietorship, and little upkeep as well. Other than keeping track of expenses and profits, the individual who owns the business need only worry about running the business rather than trying to document every detail of the business's functioning.

The disadvantages include the following:

1) Raising money to start a sole proprietorship is more difficult than in other business setup scenarios. You essentially rely on your own private capital to create this type of business unless you can find other resources, so starting off the business with enough capital can be challenging.

2) There is no such thing as limited liability with a sole proprietorship. Any losses to the business come out of the pocket of the owner if the business does not have the funding to cover them. That is, the owner is personally responsible to pay any debt the business owes.

3) A sole proprietorship is a heavy burden to bear. The owner runs the business and is responsible for everything that concerns the business, including taxes, legal responsibilities, operational tasks, and hiring and managing employees, among other things.

To summarize, the sole proprietorship places a heavy burden of responsibility and liability on the owner to fund and run the business, but in return allows the owner more flexibility in running the business and gives a bit of a break on tax preparation.

Cooperative

A cooperative operates for the benefit of the consumers, such that the business is run for the sake of the users of the given product or service. This is a special type of business that must meet certain qualifications in order to receive the tax break benefits to which cooperatives are privy.

The benefits of a cooperative are these:

1) The taxation on a cooperative is less than other types of businesses. This is because the business operates for the sake of the consumer rather than purely for profit. This is one of the reasons that the classification as a cooperative is more restrictive.

2) Funding opportunities are easier than in a sole proprietorship because you have more investors pooling their resources. This means that financial burden does not just fall on one person.

3) Because of decreased taxes and other ways to reduce costs, you can increase the quality of the products and services that you are providing through your cooperative.

4) Perpetual existence is one advantage that cooperatives have over LLCs. LLCs cease to exist if one or more of the members decides to leave the LLC. With a cooperative, members can come and go as they please and the cooperative business will continue to exist.

5) Cooperatives are democratic organizations, so they necessarily serve the needs of the members. This means that cooperatives are run by the members for the members' purposes.

The drawbacks to a cooperative are these:

1) It is difficult to obtain capital from investors. Investors do not usually look at cooperatives as potentially lucrative investments and so, unless there are personal reasons they support the cooperative, they will usually refrain from giving financial investment to a start-up cooperative.

2) Because this type of business structure is democratic, a lack of membership participation can really hurt the cooperative. That is, if the members do not show up and vote, a quorum cannot be established and no decisions can be made. Decisions take longer to process in a democratic organization such as this.

In summary, the cooperative reduces costs but must operate in a specific manner to qualify for the tax breaks that it is allowed. It is more flexible that the LLC in that members may come and go without ending the business, but it must be a democratic organization.

Corporation (C Corporation)

A corporation is an independent legal entity that is owned by shareholders. The corporation is liable for any losses that it takes rather than the shareholders. This is a much more complex structure for a business than the other structures, and comes with these advantages:

1) There is limited liability for the owners of the company, also known as the shareholders. The company itself, as its own legal entity, is responsible for any debts that accumulate, so the shareholders and owners of the company are not responsible for assuming these as losses.

2) There is the built-in ability of the corporation to generate capital through selling stock. Individuals or

groups of people will purchase stock in a corporation and thereby lend capital to the corporation as it is starting up, or whenever the main shareholders who are also the owners sell stock.

3) Corporations also receive corporate tax treatment so that the company's losses and profits are filed separately from the expenses and wages of the individual owner or owners. This separate filing allows owners to not pay taxes on what they do not receive from the company.

4) Employees generally like to work for corporations more often. Corporations are seen as having greater benefits and stability for the employees. Because the company is not tied to the financial stability of an individual but rather to the company itself, there is less fluctuation in the business than some other models of business.

Some of the disadvantages of the corporation are as follows:

1) A corporation is very costly to establish in terms of time as well as monetary capital. It is time-consuming to get all the paperwork together to establish a corporation and will cost you a good amount in legal fees to be sure that you are setting the business up correctly. A corporation is also very costly to maintain and run, again, both time-wise and financially.

2) With some corporations, double-taxing occurs on the profits of the company. That is, the profits are taxed once under the corporation and then again when they are liquidated to become dividends to the shareholders. This double taxing is a big turnoff to many people, but there are possibly some ways around it with an S-type corporation.

3) Corporations require a lot of extra paperwork, including tax forms and other record-keeping upkeep. This places a burden of time-consuming work, and

requires a dedicated financial and record-keeping manager in many cases.

Essentially, a corporation provides a greater sense of stability to the owners, shareholders, and employees by limiting the liability of the individual parties so that the responsibility for debts lies on the corporation itself. In exchange, you will sacrifice efficiency and ease of management for the complex paperwork and regulations that you must follow as a corporation.

Partnerships

There are a few types of partnerships, the most popular of which is a *general partnership.* A general partnership functions much like a sole proprietorship, just with two or more owners. A *limited partnership* limits the liability of the parties involved, just as well as an LLC would limit them. A *joint venture* is a general partnership that lasts for a set amount of time, after which point it may decide to become a general partnership or any other kind of business model.

We will discuss the advantages and disadvantages of the general partnership only since this is the type of partnership that is most common. The benefits of a general partnership are these:

1) This is the easiest and most inexpensive option for multiple partners who want open a company together. A general partnership requires the least amount of paperwork for a multiple-owner company, and has the smoothest transition from an idea on paper to a legal business entity. That is, the paperwork is nearly negligible to establish a general partnership.

2) Another advantage of the general partnership is the shared financial commitment of the partners, which is often written up in a legally signed contract.

3) Unlike a sole proprietorship, general partnerships can take advantage of complementary skillsets among the partners. That is, one might be a great financial planner, and another a wonderful operations manager, while another has skill in the specific line of work in which the business is based. These skills can all come together for the good of the company in a general partnership.

4) There exists in a general partnership, incentives for the employees to work hard and invest in the company: the employees could become partners in the company as well. This opportunity, if presented to the employees, will cause them to invest more energy in their work so that they might have a greater share in the profits of the business.

Some disadvantages to forming a general partnership are these:

1) There exists both joint and individual liability in the general partnership for any debts or costs related to the company. This means that the company as a whole is liable and responsible to pay any debts, but if the company defaults, the individual partners are held legally responsible to pay the debts.

2) Unlike in a sole proprietorship, general partnerships leave room for disagreement between partners. This is a problem because it makes running the business less smooth of a process, with each partner having equal weight in making a decision. This could send a mixed message to the employees, the consumer base, or the public and diminishes the efficiency of the company's procedures.

3) In addition to allowing room for partners to disagree, the partners must also share the profits of the ventures they make. Sole proprietorship means that the sole proprietor, or owner, keeps the profits of the company, but a general partnership necessarily splits

the profits between the partners that invested to create the company, resulting in less for each partner.

A general partnership is one of the easiest types of business models to set up, but it leaves the owners, or partners, exposed and vulnerable to liability and personal responsibility for any debts the company owes. This business model of a general partnership gives the benefit of combining the skills of various partners at the risk of partner disagreements.

S Corporation

This type of corporation is named for one of the federal laws that governs it, stipulations about it being in a certain section S. It is a special type of corporation in which the business itself it not taxed, but instead everything for taxes passes through the individual members of the company. Profits and losses are figured through the owners of the company at a lower tax rate than if the profits were taxed separately as part of the corporation or were double taxed.

There is a stipulation for this benefit, which is that the members must pay themselves a "fair wage" according to federal standards, or else part of the profits will be taxed as wages instead of as profits through the individual member or members.

The advantage of the S corporation lies in the following traits:

1) There are tax savings compared to if the taxes were taken through the corporation or if they were double taxed, through the corporation and then through the individual once it is split into dividends. This means more money for the individual member or members.

2) If a business is set up as an S corporation, because the profits are figured through the individual members'

personal tax forms, business expense tax credits can be figured into the taxes. This reduces the amount of taxes that you will have to pay on the profits that your business makes.

3) This type of business setup gives the corporation independent life, such that the business does not die if a member leaves the corporation, since the shareholders own the business. This is more flexible than the LLC model and allows the members greater freedom to come and go as they please.

Some of the disadvantages of an S corporation are as follows:

1) There are much stricter operational procedures for the S corporation than for a general partnership or LLC. Someone in the company, if not multiple people, will need to learn about these procedures and regulations in order to ensure that the company is legal and abides but the federal and state laws of the land.

2) Shareholders must be compensated fairly in this model, such that the members who own and work for the company are required to have a fair wage. If this does not happen, the IRS will likely take some of the profits of the company and tax them as wages to make up for the difference.

To summarize, the S corporation gives the benefits of tax savings to the shareholders, or owners of the company. This is accomplished through passing the profits through the individual owners on their personal tax form. This comes at the price of the shareholder compensation requirements, which designates that a certain amount must be paid to the owners who work for the company. In addition, this model gives independent life to the business, since it is a corporation, but comes at the cost of stricter operational processes.

A tempting option for many business owners is to combine the LLC with the S corporation. This combines the benefits of the LLC with the tax benefits of the S corporation while negating some of the drawbacks of the LLC.

What is an LLC?

An LLC, or limited liability company, treats its owners as members, like a cooperative, rather than as shareholders, like a corporation. The LLC is not a separate legal entity that is taxed separately from the members, but rather the profits and losses pass through each member's tax filings. Thus, an LLC is taxed like a partnership rather than like a corporation.

Additionally, the LLC does *not* have independent life but rather is dependent on the members, so if one member leaves for whatever reason, the LLC ceases to exist.

As mentioned before, the LLC can be combined with the S corporation to mitigate some of the disadvantages of the LLC. In the next chapter, we will look more specifically at the benefits and drawbacks of an LLC in comparison and contrast to the other business models.

Chapter 2: Benefits and Drawbacks of the LLC

In this chapter, we will take a look at the specific advantages and disadvantages of the LLC, and discover ways to negate the disadvantages of the LLC to make it the perfect business model for your company. We will also look at how to use the benefits to your advantage as we go through and discuss them.

<u>ADVANTAGES</u>

First, let us investigate the benefits of the limited liability company.

Limited Liability

Limited liability protects the members of the limited liability company from being responsible for the debts of the company on a personal level. That is, if the company is sued or for some reason must default on a debt, the debt is not the responsibility of the members but rather the LLC goes into bankruptcy as an entity in and of itself. This makes the LLC safer for the members than a general partnership or sole proprietorship. Instead of debts passing through the owners, the liability remains with the company so that each owner's personal assets are safe in the case of a financial difficulty or worse, monetary catastrophe, within the company.

This is similar to the corporation and the S corporation, and thus makes the LLC compatible with the S corporation. Thus, if you are looking for limited liability, the LLC or the corporation, both of which are treated as an independent entity in terms of liability and responsibility for debts, are the best options.

Less Record Keeping

Unlike the corporation, which is highly regulated by the local, state, and federal governments, the LLC does not have as many legal stipulations attached to it. That is, the paperwork involved in creating, or establishing, and maintaining, or running, an LLC are much less than you would see with a corporation.

Instead of keeping track of all the business profits, losses, liquidated dividends, wages to the owners, and many other things, you need only track the business profits and losses, as these all run through the members' tax filings as one large total.

This makes the LLC similar to the general partnership and sole proprietorship. Instead of tracking the business profits and shareholder dividends separately, the profits are taken as a total and run through the member's personal tax filings in total. Additionally, other regulations, such as a fair wage for the shareholders, do not exist for the LLC, just as they do not for the general partnership and sole proprietorship, making these entities easier to run and maintain than the C corporations and S corporations.

Tax Advantages

The LLC has the advantage of only being taxed once, through the members' personal tax filings, instead of twice, as such profits would be in a C corporation. Instead of being taxed once as a corporation and again as dividends through the shareholders, LLC's tax filings are simply figured through the personal filings of the members one time.

This is the main advantage of the general partnership, the sole proprietorship, and the LLC over the C corporation. Being taxed twice on profit can seriously diminish the amount of money that goes into the owners' pockets. To avoid this, one can create an LLC instead of a corporation, passing the taxes through their own personal filing in order to cut down on the amount of taxes taken out of the total profits.

Flexibility of Ownership

In an LLC, the number and type of owners is not limited by regulations like the S corporation. This means that the LLC might have more owners than an S corporation is allowed, and it might have owners that are corporations rather than just individuals. The S corporation allows for pass-through taxation but limits the number and type of owners to 100 or less individuals. On the other hand, if you have more than 100 people involved, or if you require that a corporation be part of the ownership of the company, then you will want to choose an LLC over an S corporation.

Flexibility of Management

LLC owners have more choices about how they want to run their business. Unlike the corporation, which is required to have a board of directors that is elected every year by the shareholders in a democratic vote based on how many shares are owned in the company, the LLC does not have a required business model. It is not regulated by the local, state, or federal government to have a specific structure of management.

The amount of regulations on corporations is a turnoff to many business owners, and the LLC provides a good number of benefits without the structural requirements and regulations of the corporation.

Flexible Sharing of Profits

While two owners might own a share in the company that is 50% each, the profits are not required to be distributed in a 50/50 fashion. If one of the members contributed more capital or time to the business at the beginning, the members might decide together that they will distribute 60% of the profits to that member and 40% to the other member. This flexibility does not exist in corporations, which is governed by the amount of stock or shares that each owner holds.

DISADVANTAGES

The disadvantages of an LLC are far outweighed by its advantages in many cases, and where they are not, filing as an S corporation can usually negate the drawbacks of the LLC.

Limited Life

Generally, an LLC is meant to last for a while, unlike the joint venture type of partnership which is created for a set period of time. This makes it an unfortunate thing when a member leaves the LLC, as this dissolves the business entity. It can then be recreated from the remaining members or with new members, but the process must be started from the beginning again when a member leaves.

This unfortunate aspect of LLC's can be possibly negated by combining the LLC with the S corporation, such that you are running an LLC with S corporation regulations. This will designate the business with an independent life of the corporation rather than being dependent on the members' staying a part of the business. Thus, the members will have greater freedom to come and go as they please.

Self-Employment Taxes

In an LLC, the profits of the business are figured through the members' personal tax filings as self-employment wages. This means that they are taxed at the higher self-employment rate. Unfortunately, even if the members do not dissolve and liquidate the profits into dividends for themselves, they are still taxed on them as though they had, meaning greater tax payments during tax season, or quarterly if you decide to file quarterly.

The reason this happens is because the IRS automatically designates an LLC as a general partnership or sole proprietorship, depending on how many members there are in the LLC. You can, however, choose to file as a C corporation (not always recommendable) or as an S corporation (usually recommendable).

Filing as a C corporation will get you caught in the trap of double taxing at times. First, the company's profits will be taxed as a corporation, and then any wages or dividends you received from the company will be taxed. You can see why this might not be recommended.

Filing as an S corporation keeps your company profits and private wages separate, taxing them each once. You are taxed at the self-employment rate for any dividends or wages you received from the business, and then the profits of the company are run through your personal tax filing in a separate category such that they are taxed at a lower rate than the self-employment rate. This is a way around the higher self-employment tax rate as an LLC, but it comes with the stipulation that you must pay yourself and your members a fair wage according to federal standards. Otherwise, more will be taken from the company profits portion and be taxed as self-employment wages, and you might incur penalties for filing incorrectly.

OVERALL RESULTS: Who can benefit?

The LLC is an optimal business setup for many businesses, perhaps including your own. If you are looking for limited liability in a high-risk business, or you are wanting to protect your personal assets from the debts of the business, then you will like the limited liability of the LLC structure.

If you do not want to hire a record keeper, or if you do not want to have to keep track of the many regulations that bind a corporation, you will like the LLC as well. It will allow you greater flexibility in that you will not have so many rules by which your company must abide.

There are tax advantages to building an LLC versus a corporation, mostly in the fact that you can avoid double taxation. Running all of the taxes through the personal tax filing of the members of the LLC instead of through the corporation and then through the individuals as dividends, is a way that you can put more money in your pocket.

Flexible ownership of an LLC is another advantage which you might like to use to your benefit. This will allow corporations and any number of owners to become a member in the LLC. This gives you greater flexibility to include various groups or parties of people that you would not otherwise be able to include.

Another advantage you will enjoy with the LLC versus a corporation is the flexibility of management. You do not have to maintain a board of directors with an LLC, so you will not waste as much time in making decisions and in simply voting in a board every year.

Finally, the last benefit to having an LLC is the flexible distribution of profits. This will allow you more options in terms of distributing the dividends of the company, such that you are not bound by law to give a certain amount to one member and a specific portion to another member. If one member owns a specific portion of the business but another regularly does more of the work, the LLC is a great option because it allows members to negotiate among themselves how the profits will be divided.

The major disadvantages can become advantages when paired with an S corporation business setup. The first major drawback is the limited life of an LLC. If any member were to leave a limited liability company, then the LLC would cease to exist and would need to be reformed or started as a different type of company. This leads to a feeling of instability within the LLC, especially when there tends to be conflict among the members.

To combat this disadvantage, you need simply to pair the LLC with an S corporation model. This means that you will have independent life of the corporation. It will allow members to leave and come as they choose by simply buying stock, or shares, in the company.

The second disadvantage, the self-employment tax on all the profits of the company, can also be negated by partnering the S corporation model with the LLC model. This allows the profits that are not wages to be taxed at a lower rate than the profits that turn into dividends. This allows more money to flow through the business itself.

Chapter 3: Choosing a Location and Name

In considering whether to establish your business as an LLC, it is helpful to know the process of setting up a limited liability company. There is a series of steps through which you must work in order to establish an LLC, but they can be explained simply enough. In order to be sure that you have the information you need, we will take the following chapter to introduce how exactly to set up a limited liability company.

Step One: Choose Your State/Location

When establishing your LLC, you will want to pay attention to individual state laws in which you are setting up your business. Many states have different regulations and requirements for filing the limited liability company status of a business. Delaware, for example, has a well-developed law system surrounding LLC's and businesses, while some states require greater fees for filing, such as California requiring upwards of $800 to file for an LLC status.

If you are operating in a particular state or are based in a particular state, this will more than likely be the state in which you register your business. If you do business in more than one state, then you might have to register in each state in which you are doing business, depending on how the laws are set up in each state. A notice to the Secretary of State is typically in order to register your LLC, and there are fees related to filing such a notice to the various Secretaries of State.

If you have a choice about which state in which you would like to set up your business, we will have some information about particular state fees and other information which you would consider in making such a decision available later in this book.

Step Two: Choose a Name

Naming an LLC might be more complex of a business than you would originally imagine it to be. Following are a list of considerations you must make when you are naming your limited liability company.

1) Typically, the name of the company needs to end with the words, "Limited Liability Company," the abbreviation, "LLC," or any other *permitted* representation of the fact that this company is, in fact, an LLC.

2) No other company filed with the Secretary of State in the state where you are filing can have the same name as your business. This includes all active foreign companies as well as any active domestic companies such that you must be sure that your name is completely unique in the state where it is registered. In California, there is an option to search LLC names on record, which you can find by heading to: https://businesssearch.sos.ca.gov/

   Again, be sure that your name is unique, not only in one state but in all the states where you might be doing business in case you must register in every state according to its laws.

3) Certain terms are prohibited by state law, such as the words, "bank," "trustee," and "insurance company." You cannot include any of these words or phrases in your company name.

4) The LLC cannot contain the words, "incorporated" or "corporation" because this would construe that the LLC is incorporated. "Corp." is also prohibited for the same reason. Anything that would construe the LLC as a corporation is prohibited in naming the LLC.

5) Do a trademark search on uspto.gov. This will show you any trademarks that you might be violating in the process of creating your LLC. Ensuring that your

trademark is unique is vital when naming your LLC to be sure it is a legal naming.

6) Search the Internet for the proposed name of your company to see if any other companies are using the same name or similar enough names that your companies might be confused. Try to avoid these names because they will cause frustration for your customers and consumer base.

7) Think future-focus. If you plan to grow beyond the town in which you are based, do not name the company after the town, for example. Naming your business "Dallas Salon, LLC" will turn away future consumers and customers that are outside the Dallas area.

8) Check on the availability of the associated website domain name that you would propose to accompany your business name. Try to find a name that has an available ".com" website domain rather than ".org" or ".net," as these latter two often cause confusion among consumers and customers trying to locate your web address.

9) Remember that you can always use one name publicly and one name formally, such as "Robert McConnell's Tire Shop of Dallas-Fort Worth, LLC" as the formal name but "Bob's Tires" as the public name by which most of your consumers will know the business. You might be required, in this case, to file "fictitious business name" paperwork or a DBA statement, "doing business as." This would be an extra step in your process, but fictitious names are not bound by the same laws as the LLC, meaning you can have the same fictitious name as another company. This is a work around if you want the public to know your company by a certain name but the limited liability company name is already taken in your state of business.

Chapter 4: Writing Articles of Organization and an Operating Agreement

The next two steps include a bit of paperwork and thought as to how you would like to run your business. The first of the two next steps begins the process of registering your limited liability company with the state (or states) in which you will be doing business. The second of two steps gives your company a structure and organization by which it will run.

Step Three: File Articles of Organization

The next step after choosing a name for the company or business that you hope to establish is to file the Articles of Organization of your business. Most states require that this document be filed with the Secretary of State of whatever state in which the business headquarters is located, or if business is conducted in that state.

The articles often include the following in the order stated:

1) The first article is the **name** of the proposed company, including the "L.L.C." or other designation as a limited liability company.

2) The second article includes both the **principal and mailing addresses** of the company. That is, if there is a principal office for the company, its address should be put first and the mailing address for the company should follow.

3) The third article designates the **registered agent and his or her address**. The registered agent is the person to whom legal communication is made in the event of a subpoena or something of the sort. This can be a member of the company, or certain companies provide registered agents to LLC's for a yearly or

monthly fee. If you are hiring the registered agent, make sure to obtain his or her street address and include it with the third article under his or her name. If the agent is one of the members, have the member give his or her current street address in the articles of organization.

4) The fourth article is the **registered agent's statement of acceptance**. This is the registered agent's acknowledgment of his or her responsibility and signature accepting the responsibilities as registered agent to receive and respond to legal contact by other entities outside the company or from within the company.

5) The fifth article is optional, as it states the **duration** of the LLC if the company is for some reason on a time clock. If this is a joint venture type of business in which the members want limited liability, they will designate an amount of time for which the LLC will last and when it will end.

6) The sixth article is about the **management** of the company. It designates the management structure of the company, though it does not specify a person or individual in charge of managing the company so as not to limit the company to one manager.

7) The seventh article lists the **members and their addresses**, including all the members that will be part of the limited liability company and the addresses at which they can be found. This does not specify the percentage owned by each of the members, but only their names and addresses.

8) The eighth article specifies the **initial contribution** by each of the members to the company, thus giving an indication of how many shares the individual or corporation holds in the company. If someone gave 45% of the initial startup capital of the company, then they own 45% of the company.

9) The ninth article indicates **purpose** of the business. This should be a rather vague and inclusive statement, such as "to conduct any and all lawful business for which Limited Liability Companies can be organized..." This allows the company to grow and expand tangentially. Perhaps your business if only selling tires at first, but later begins installing tires and eventually becomes a full auto-repair shop. If your articles of organization state your business "is pursuing the sale of tires to owners of vehicles throughout the county," you cannot legally begin the installation of tires and especially cannot open a full auto repair shop.

10) The tenth article is the **liability** clause. This clause puts the responsibility for "debts, obligations, or other liabilities" on the limited liability company alone. It specifically points out that the members and managers of the company are *not* responsible for these things listed: debts, obligations, or other liabilities.

11) The eleventh article states who is the **organizer** of the Articles of Organization, that is, who drew up the Articles of Organization. It contains the date on which the Articles were signed as well, followed by the organizer's signature and contact information.

These articles are then mailed in with the appropriate fee to the Secretary of State for the specific state in which you are opening the company. Some states have pre-written forms with fillable spaces for your company's information available online, and some of these also require you indicate the management style of your company: whether it will be by one manager, multiple managers, or by all members of the LLC.

Step Four: Write an LLC Operating Agreement

The operating agreement is a set of rules to which the members agree, and sign to establish as the operational standards by which the limited liability company will run. Here is a list with a general order in which the articles of operation might occur:

1) The **name** of the limited liability company will appear first at the top of the first page.

2) The **certificate of formation** (otherwise called the articles of organization) is included as proof that an LLC was in fact formed by the members legally with the state or states. This is good record-keeping.

3) The name of the **registered agent** as well as the address and contact information for his or her office must be included.

4) The **term of the LLC** will be established with the stipulations given for how the LLC would cease to function as an LLC, such as if a member leaves the membership.

5) The **voting rights** of the members will be established. This will specify how much of the vote each member has, if it is not a democratic system with each person having one vote. It might be by shares the member has in the company, such that someone with 20% of the investment in the company has 20% of the voting power.

6) This will include the **business purpose** of the company. Again, you want to make the statement broad enough to include expansion of the business, but you should be more specific than you were with the articles of organization. This statement will shape how you run the business and your goals as a company, so take a while to think through the statement.

7) The **principal place of business** will be defined by this document, so the address of the headquarters of

the company will be included in the operating agreement.

8) This document will give instructions for the incorporation of **new members** into the business. It will answer the questions of how new members are chosen by the current members and how they are admitted into the group.

9) The operating agreement includes a list of the initial contributors and how much each of them contributed. It is a record of the members' investment in the company and specifically says that no more will be required of the business members to start the business, though there might be later contributions.

10) This document will instruct the members going forward about what the LLC will do with its **profits** and how it will handle its **losses**. This tells the company how to handle various situations and will guide the members' behavior in those situations.

11) The operating agreement will have a clause about how the LLC makes **distributions**. This means that is guides the members in how they will liquidate the profits that the company has accumulated, and in how they will divide the profits among the members once liquidated.

12) There will be a point that dictates to **the manager** or managers of the company how he or she will **run the company**. It does not get into the specifics of the rights of the manager or his or her powers, as that is a separate clause.

13) This point dictates the **powers of the managers and of the members**. It talks about the rights of the manager and what actions he or she can or cannot take in running the business. It lists the powers of the members as well: when, how, and why the members

may step in to help handle various situations or overrule the manager in a decision.

14) Another clause will talk about **how the limited liability company will maintain its records**. This clause dictates how the records will be made, where and how they will be stored, and how to access the records.

15) There will, of course, be a clause outlining the **rights of the members**. This assigns certain rights, like the right to take distributions individually, separate from the other members, and the rights to other such actions to the members individually and as a group.

There may be other subjects you would like to address in the operating agreement, such as the procedure in the event of the dissolution of the LLC, the process for indemnification of a member, procedures for any meetings that are held, and how the voting rights are distributed. Be thorough in thinking about the running of your business. Think about what you want a typical day to look like, a typical week, a typical month, and a typical year, and this will help you think about what subjects you need to address in the operating agreement.

Once you have completed the LLC's operating agreement, it must be signed by all the members and the managers. This signifies that the members and the managers approve of and consent to abide by the terms of the operating agreement. Store this in a safe place and provide copies to all your members and managers.

Chapter 5: Raising Capital and Obtaining Proper Licensing

Before you can run your LLC, you will need to raise the capital necessary for the startup, as well as obtain the Employer Identification Number (EIN) and the necessary licensing to run your business. First, we will discuss raising capital for your business, and then, we will learn about how to obtain an EIN and proper licensing.

Raising Capital

There are a few types of investors in which you might be interested. First, there are family members. You will know best how to approach your family member with a request for investment, whether it be formally with your business plan in hand, or informally with a simple explanation of your endeavor and beseeching for their help.

The other types of investors are angel investors and venture capital financers. These types of investors require a different type of convincing. We will now discuss some tips on pitching angel investors and venture capitals.

1) **Obtain referrals and references**. Do not end your executive summary or business plan unsolicited. This will turn off the investor because investors receive hundreds of such emails and paper mailings. Having a reference or referral to another current investor included will give the potential new investor confidence, and provide them a third party with which they can discuss the business.

2) **Find an investor interested in your type of work**. That is, seek out and do some homework on the various investors in your area or across the country who invest in your type of work specifically.

This will increase your chances of obtaining the investment.

3) **Make it simple and concise**. Make sure the business plan or executive review that you submit to the investor is short and sweet. Respect his or her time and you might receive inquiries for further information, which you can submit at that time, rather than giving all the information upfront.

4) **Be realistic**. Do not tell the investor that you do not foresee any competition or use clichés like, "the product will market itself." Do not pretend there are not risks in your business.

5) **Everyone who comes to present to the investor should have a speaking role**. Make sure that if you bring someone, he or she is there for a reason. Do not bring your team if only you will do the speaking.

6) **Have a marketing strategy ready to present**. Talk about how you plan to market your product or service.

7) **Be specific about how you will use the investment capital.** This will make the investor more at ease that you are not just throwing the capital away, but instead that you have a specific plan to use it wisely.

Should you obtain investors, you will need to outline how investments will work and what benefit investors will receive from the LLC. You will lay this out in the Articles of Organization and possibly in an investor rights agreement. Remember that it is not as likely to find angel investors and venture capitals who invest in LLCs, but it *is* possible to find them if you look hard. If you need investors, this is good advice for pitching the potential man, woman, or company that your new LLC is worth the investment.

Obtain an Employer Identification Number (EIN)

You will obtain an EIN, also known as a Federal Tax Identification Number, through filing the IRS Form SS-4. Filling out the paperwork with pen and paper will take a few minutes, but waiting for the paperwork to process will take at least a few weeks. If you would like to speed up the process, look on the IRS website and find the application for an Employer Identification Number, which you can access here: https://www.irs.gov/businesses/small-businesses-self-employed/apply-for-an-employer-identification-number-ein-online

You will need the following information to fill out the SS-4 paperwork:

1) Legal name of the business

2) Trade name (operating name) of the business

3) Executor, administrator, trustee, "care of" name under which the business is filing for an EIN

4) Mailing address

5) Street address (principal address)

6) County and state in which the principal business is located

7) Name and Social Security Number of the responsible party

8) Number of members of the LLC

9) The type of business as which you will file taxes (sole proprietorship, partnership, corporation, etc.)

10) Reason for applying for an EIN – check the "started new business" box

11) Date the business started

12) Closing month of the accounting year

13) How many employees you expect to hire in the next year

14) First date that wages or annuities were paid

15) The line of business of your company

16) Any previous EIN's for the same company

You will need an EIN in order to open a business bank account. Otherwise, everything must run through a personal bank account, which is not recommended.

Business Licenses

There might be local, state, or federal business license for various types of businesses. For example, selling firearms will require federal and state business licenses. Many big cities, like San Francisco and Chicago, require licensing for many types of businesses, such as retail stores, restaurants, theaters, daycares, manufacturing facilities and motor vehicle repair shops.

Be sure to do your homework and look up your type of business in your local city, county, state, and federal jurisdiction to see if you need any special licensing. This will often cost another fee to apply for and obtain the specific license. Take this into account when raising your capital.

Chapter 6: Bank Accounts, Membership Ledgers and Keeping Current with Filings

As you raise capital, you will want a more legitimate place to put the capital than into your private bank account. Investors would not look kindly on you taking their money and putting it in a private, individual account. You will also want to keep track of the ownership of the company on a membership ledger, and finally, you will need to keep up with current filings of information that can cause fees or penalties if not met.

Establishing a Bank Account

In order to create credibility and legitimacy for your company and to make expenses and profits easier to track, you will want to open a business bank account. A business account is different than a personal account and is attached to the Employer Identification Number, or EIN, that you just obtained online or through filing by mail.

Then, you will want to weigh your options for bank accounts. Some things to consider when you look at various accounts at different banks are as follows:

1) How much do checks cost? Will you be using a check card, also known as a debit card, or will you primarily use checks to make your payments for the upkeep of the company? If checks are very costly in one instance and not in another, and you plan to pay bills exclusively by check, you could save money by going with the account that gives you less expensive check books.

2) What options does the account or bank offer for running transactions for your business? There are often merchant services that allow you to take credit and debit card transactions, but these services can

cost a good amount. Check with your potential bank to see how much their merchant services cost.

3) What kinds of fees are there on the account type that you would like to open? Are these reasonable for your type of business? Figure in the fees to your monthly budget and see if it is reasonably affordable or wise to open up the type of account that you are considering.

4) What are the benefits of the accounts at which you are looking? Some have free or discounted merchant services. Some have free checks. Check out the benefits of the accounts so that you can choose the account that gives your company the most useful advantages.

5) What requirements do the accounts have? Many times, accounts require a minimum balance to be maintained or a minimum number of debit card transactions to be made on the account. Make sure that you can maintain the balance or transaction number before you open the account or you will incur fees.

6) Is there any interest on the account? This is more relevant for savings than for checking accounts, but generally, the higher the minimum balance of the account, the higher the percentage of interest you receive. If you do not maintain the balance, however, you will incur a fee that will likely eat away at the small profits you were making through having interest on the account.

7) How convenient are the hours and the location? Can you reasonably get to the bank in time during the week during business hours, or does it possibly have weekend or evening hours? Take these things into consideration when choosing a bank account.

Once you do choose a bank and bank account type, make sure that you have your Employer Identification Number and other information ready for the banker to reference in creating the account. The bank might want to see your other paperwork as well, such as the articles of organization, or your operating procedures with the clause stating you will open a bank account. Bring enough to make an opening deposit as well. The amount of an opening deposit varies by bank, so call ahead and do your research to be sure you bring the correct amount in cash or as a check.

Membership Ledger

You will keep a membership ledger as a means of keeping track of who owns how much of the company. This is a simpler version of a stock ledger, which records the shareholders and their number of shares, plus when the shares were acquired.

Likewise, the membership ledger will show the transfer or units of the business between the members. It will keep a record of the number of units, the type of units, and the date the units were transferred, as well as to whom they were transferred, and who from. The membership ledger is very important for keeping track of changes in the business' ownership. While a member leaving and giving up all of his or her units would result in the dissolution of the limited liability company, the transfer of ownership of units of the company without a member leaving lets the LLC remain intact.

Keep Current with Filings

Annually, there are report filings due for an LLC called the yearly LLC update forms. Make sure you keep current with these because you can be fined or penalized otherwise, up to the point of suspension or dissolution of your company.

This will become more complex of a job when you begin to expand into different states, since different states have different paperwork and different deadlines. Pay attention to the filing dates and paperwork in each state in which you do business to maintain the legality of your business, and to ensure you will avoid penalties, fines, suspension, and dissolution of your LLC in that state.

Chapter 7: Legal Obligations of an LLC

The limited liability company is legally responsible for certain actions and consequences that come with running a business. These responsibilities include debt, profit distributions, employee activities, and tax reporting.

Debt

The limited liability company takes responsibility for any debt in which the company finds itself. If there is a legal debt, such that someone sued the company for a negative impact at the company's hands, the company is liable to pay that debt.

The only time the members are liable to pay the debt is if they were personally involved. For example, the company might not have a great credit score, and as such, the owner of the company guaranteed payment on a loan personally using his or her own credit score. Then, if the company becomes unable to pay the debt, the owner becomes personally responsible to pay it. Also, if the member of the LLC personally injured someone on company grounds, the member would become personally responsible.

Profit Distributions

Many states have adopted some form of the Uniform Limited Liability Company Act, which allows LLCs to not divide the profits entirely, but to keep some within the company bank account. The operating agreement might designate an amount that above which the profits are divided among the owners. This must be abided by to stay legal, so make sure to create internal laws by which you can abide in your operating agreement.

Employee Actions

Because the LLC is a separate legal entity, it may hire employees to work for it. It is then responsible for these employees' actions while they are on the job.

For example, is a pizza delivery driver cuts off another car and that car goes crashing into the center rails, the *company* is liable to pay the damages and hospital bills for the injured party or parties. Of course, this is to be taken within reason. If the delivery driver had a personal vendetta against the other driver and, in anger, drove to push the other driver off the road, then the delivery driver and not the LLC is responsible, since it is a personal dispute at that point.

Tax Reporting

The company is liable and responsible to report taxes yearly or quarterly, depending on the situation. We will discuss this more in the next chapter, the specifics of which are relevant to any LLC that is created anywhere in the country.

Keeping Information on File

On file must be the business **name and address**, along with other contact information for the business. Also, you must have the contact information and name of the **registered agent** of the company, whether it be a hired agent or one of the members.

Additionally, you need to have the **operating agreement** which you signed with all the members and managers, as well as the various **business licenses and permits** from the local, county, state, and federal governments. Some states, including California, require a **statement of information** with the above information, such as name, address, contact information, registered agent's name and contact information, and the Employer Identification Number (EIN).

You need to keep your current and past ***tax forms*** on file as well, in addition to the ***articles of organization*** that you filed with the Secretary of State or other governmental party appropriate to your state's way of running LLC legal business. You will need your ***local licenses and registration***, such as your city registration, handy.

Yearly update forms are required to be on file with your LLC business as well.

Financial Obligations

You are expected to pay yearly filing and maintenance fees for your LLC. Filing the yearly LLC update forms will require a fee be paid. Filing and paying taxes is also required.

If you would like your business to succeed, it is good to have at least one member or manager who can keep track of all the deadlines, filings, and fees that must be paid.

Chapter 8: LLC Taxes

The limited liability company must pay a variety of taxes. You will have to pay attention to various state laws in collecting and paying these taxes, especially if you are operating in multiple states. You will want some robust financial software or a person with strong skills in keeping track of many moving parts to help you in managing the tax part of the LLC.

First, let's take a look at federal taxes. After that we can talk about how to estimate taxes for the federal portion of your tax, and then we will discuss sales taxes and then finally state taxes.

Federal Income Taxes – Single-Owner LLC

If you are the only owner or member of your limited liability company, the Internal Revenue Service, or IRS, will automatically classify and tax your business as a sole proprietorship. This means that you will not be taxed as a business, but rather as an individual through self-reported, self-employment income. All profits and losses are "passed through" your personal income tax form.

You will need Form 1040 to complete your taxes as a result. You will report all the profits and losses on the 1040 form as though they happened to you rather than to your business. Any amount the company cost you becomes a business expense and any profit becomes income. You cannot bypass this by refusing to dissolve the assets that you have accumulated, or by keeping the capital that has built up in the company account. Even if the money remains in the company bank account, it is still figured through your personal tax return.

You will also use the Schedule C form in doing your taxes, as this is the form for sole proprietorship businesses. Be careful not to use Schedule E, which is for Supplemental Income or Loss, or Schedule F, which is for Farming Income or Loss. Schedule C is specifically built for sole proprietorships and LLCs with a single owner, and your taxes will be rejected if you use the wrong forms.

As for which federal identification number you could use, most often you will be filling in your personal Social Security number rather than your Employer Identification Number. The EIN is more for the use of the employees when reporting their wages. Some states will have you use the EIN in place of the Social Security number, so read carefully depending on which form you are filling out.

Federal Income Taxes – Multi-Member LLC

Like the single-owner LLC, the multi-member LLC, or multi-owner LLC are not taxed as separate entities, but rather as a general partnership. This means you will need the same forms as a general partnership would need to file federal taxes.

First you will use Form 1065 to divide up the profits and losses. You will do this according to the operating agreement's rules. If the operating agreement says that one member has 45% interest in the company, another 35%, and another 20%, then the first member would take 45% of the profits and 45% of the losses, the second would take 35% of the profits and 35% of the losses, and the last member would take the remaining 20% of the profits and the remaining 20% of the losses. This separating out of profits and losses *must* match on all three individuals' tax return forms, or their Form 1065s. If not, you might be subject to audit, and then to further penalties and fees.

Once you have the profits and losses divided between the members, you would then transfer the information pertaining to you to your 1040 Form. You will fill out the 1040 Form just as you would do with self-employed income. Your tax rate will be higher than an employee's tax rate because you are paying both the employer's and the employee's portion of the income tax, Medicare tax, and Social Security tax. Not to fret, you are also able to count the losses against your taxes such that any losses you experience become deductions as business expenses.

One moral of the story is that you will want to form a good, clear operating agreement. Though the operating agreement is not required by most states, it is *highly* recommended so that there are not as many issues later with dividing up the profits and losses, for example. This will decrease the chances of a major disagreement, which could cause the LLC to dissolve if a member decides to leave. Setting the expectations early and agreeing upon them is vital to the smooth running and maintenance of your business.

Filing as a Corporation

If you would like to change the way your limited liability company is treated by the Internal Revenue Service, the IRS requires that you fill out Form 8832. This will allow you to file taxes as a corporation, whether it be as a C corporation or as an S corporation.

Filing as a corporation will require extra work but will subject fewer of the profits to the high self-employment tax, and instead to the lower corporate tax. If you are leaving money in the business account rather than dividing up every penny of the profits among the members, this might be a tempting plan.

To complete the filing as a corporation, you will use the Employer Identification Number, and Form 1120. Fill out the appropriate information for the LLC on the 1120 Form, and any profits that became your earnings will go on your personal 1040 Form.

Remember, if you file as a C corporation, you might be receiving double taxation, as the total amount of profits are figured into the taxing of the company as a separate entity rather than just the portion that has remained with the company. The individual members are then taxed on their portion of the dividends, or on whatever they were provided by the company financially.

Paying Estimated Taxes

Because you are not paying taxes on the earnings that you and other members make from your business until you file taxes, you are required to file and pay estimated taxes quarterly.

To file and pay quarterly estimated taxes, you will use the 1040-ES Form to estimate your taxes. Perform the calculations that are required by the form, estimating your income from the business for the year. This will then result in a number that you should pay quarterly, on April 15, July 15, October 15, and January 15 of each year (or, if these are a holiday or a weekend, the closest business day after these days).

Make sure to pay at least the amount that is recommended by the 1040-ES Form. If you make more than you estimated, you will end up paying the remainder of what you owe on the April 15 payment. If you do not pay the right amount, you are subject to penalties and fees as well as to an audit by the IRS.

You will be paying out of your income the self-employment tax, the Social Security tax, and the Medicare tax. Depending on how much the total is that you are earning, you will pay a differing percentage of your total earnings in self-employment tax.

Sales Tax

Each state and locality has its own taxes. Some states, like Nevada, have no sales tax because their taxes come from somewhere else, such as the casinos. Other states have higher sales tax, and some localities add even more tax to the state tax due to additional services or programs being funded.

Sales tax is a point of purchase tax. The state and local governments determine the percentage of the tax, and you as a business in the state and locality will assess the amount of tax on a product or service, collect the tax along with the price of the product, and pass the tax money along to the state or local government to which it belongs.

This can get complicated if you are working in a few different states or localities that have different taxes, or even the same percentage amount of tax but you must pay the tax to various state local governments. You will again want some robust software if you are working in multiple locations, or you will want to hire someone who can keep track of the multiple pieces of relevant information in order to stay within lawful guidelines.

State Taxes

You will want to pay state taxes for the state or states in which you are operating, along with the federal taxes that you pay quarterly. Oftentimes, the state taxes will work the same as the federal taxes, taxing you and your company's members rather than the company itself by default. If you do not want to be taxed as a general partnership, each state should have its own form that you can find online to be taxed as a corporation, whether as an S corporation or as a C corporation.

Along with state taxes, you might be assessed an annual LLC fee, otherwise known as a franchise tax, a registration fee, or a renewal fee. This will be by state, so check on each state in which your LLC is registered to be sure you are paying the correct fees along with your taxes. If not, you might find you end up with penalties, more fees, suspension of your right to operate, or dissolution of your limited liability company.

Chapter 9: Bringing It All Together

The limited liability company is one of a few options that you have when you are establishing your business. If you choose to create an LLC, you'll want to make the process of establishing and maintaining it as simple as possible.

For that reason, below is a conclusive checklist of the tasks you must complete in order to create your LLC. The process is as follows:

- **Choose the state and locality in which you will establish your LLC.** Research tax laws and LLC laws in the places where you might establish your LLC, and choose the one that best fits your needs. Make sure you know the filing procedures and deadlines for your company's location. If you are operating in more than one locality or state, then be sure to keep track of all the proceedings and deadlines involved in the process of creating and maintaining your business.

- **Choose a company name.** This must end with the words "Limited Liability Company" or the acronym, "LLC" in order to be a legitimate limited liability company. Also, it must be unique in the state in which you are registering it. There are ways to look up other LLC names in some states, and in others it will be by trial and error as you send in your potential name and receive an affirmative or negative answer back from the Secretary of State.

- **File the Articles of Organization with your Secretary of State.** This will be your official notice to the state that you are seeking to create a limited liability company. The format for the Articles of Organization can be found in Chapter 4 of this book. Make sure not to limit yourself to a certain, specific area of business but leave your options open when you file the Articles of Organization, as these will govern what it is possible for your LLC to accomplish.

- **Write and sign an operating agreement**. This operating agreement will also govern how you and the other members as well as how the managers and members interact. Be sure that everyone is on the same page and agrees whole-heartedly to the operating agreement. This is crucial to the smooth running of your business.

- **Raise capital for your business**. You might have enough capital between you and the other members to begin running the business, but if not, you will need to raise capital through solicitation of angel investors and venture capital investors. Know your audiences and pitch to them according to their interests and passions.

- **Obtain an Employer Identification Number.** Again, you can easily do this online and instantly receive your EIN as soon as you fill in and submit the relevant information. If not, you can use the IRS's SS-4 Form, fill it out by hand, and submit it to the Federal Internal Revenue Service and receive a response within about a month.

- **Obtain business licenses and permits.** Some businesses require extra licensing, such as if you plan to serve alcohol or sell firearms. These permits come at the local, county, state, and federal level. Research which permits or licenses your type of business needs in your area and submit the proper paperwork to obtain that licensing.

- **Create and deposit in your business bank account**. Remember that your business bank account will add credibility and legitimacy to your business, s, while it is not required, it is generally well-recommended.

To upkeep and maintain your business you will want to do the following:

- **Keep an updated membership ledger**. This will tell you how many units of the business each member possesses, which will be important in figuring your taxes and estimated taxes that you pay quarterly, as it tells you how to divide the profits and losses of the company among its members.

- o **Keep current with filings**. Make sure that you know the deadlines for various filings, such as the yearly LLC update filing and other such reports that you must submit. Keep current with your filings to avoid hiccups in the running of your business, such as fees, penalties, suspension, or dissolution.

- o **Be sure to pay your taxes on time, and in the correct amount**. This will help so that you will not owe a large amount in April, but rather you will have taken taxes out throughout the year.

If you stick to these tips and complete this check list, you will be well on your way to having a booming new LLC business. You will have created a company with stability, where all the members are in agreement about how to run the business. You will have the capital to start up and run your business. You will have all the proper paperwork that you need to be legally safe, and you will have no surprises when it comes to tax time.

In short, you will have an excellent start to what is often a lifelong dream to start your own business. Best of luck!

Conclusion

Thanks again for taking the time to read this book!

You should now have a good understanding of limited liability companies, and be well prepared to establish your own.

If you enjoyed this book, please take the time to leave me a review on Amazon. I appreciate your honest feedback, and it really helps me to continue producing high quality books.

www.ingramcontent.com/pod-product-compliance
Lightning Source LLC
LaVergne TN
LVHW020051160726
843469LV00043B/1597